# Scuba Diving

## A short guide to open water training

Richard Devanney

Kindle Direct Publishing

Cover photo courtesy of Alex Dawson Photography
https://www.alex-dawson.com

# Contents

# Introduction

Getting certified as a scuba diver can be one of the most satisfying things you'll ever do. It's estimated that there are 6 million people around the world that enjoy diving as a hobby, and they all had to start somewhere. This guide explains exactly what a scuba diving course entails to make it easy to get started on the road to getting certified.

**Please note that this book does not in any way teach you how to dive. Diving is a practical sport that you can only learn under the supervision and guidance of a qualified scuba instructor.**

This book is not an encyclopedia on everything and anything to do with diving. It's aimed specifically at those people who have already made the decision to learn to dive. It's designed to reduce confusion about the process of getting certified.

You'll find information on which organizations provide training, how their training differs, how long a course takes, what you will do during a course, and what your options are post-course. It also provides guidance on things to consider to help you find the right course for you.

# Scuba diving- an overview

## What is scuba diving?

People have all sorts of wild ideas about what it means to be a scuba diver. It won't allow you to find Atlantis (though no harm in looking), and sadly the Titanic is a little bit deep to dive. Simply put, scuba diving involves using equipment that allows you to breathe underwater for extended periods of time.

The equipment also enables you to control how deep you go and how quickly you ascend (always slowly). Diving is always done in groups of no less than 2 people. Most people do it for fun to watch marine life and explore a small underwater area. It's a great thing to do when on vacation, but it can also be something to enjoy locally.

Recreational divers are not allowed to go very deep. The first level of training limits you to dive no deeper than 60ft (18m). The absolute deepest that is allowed with further training is 130ft (40m). Divers can go deeper than this via an advanced form of diving known as technical diving. But this is beyond the scope of this book.

The amount of time that you can spend underwater depends on how much air you take with you, how fast you breathe and how deep you go. Typical dive times for experienced divers are around an hour. New divers may get dive times of 20-40 minutes. Most divers undertake 2 dives per day and they must spend time on the surface between dives. Unsurprisingly, this is called a surface interval.

## Why learn to scuba dive?

Everyone has their own motivations for wanting to learn diving. Some want to see marine life, others like the idea of exploring new places or just doing something different. For some people, it's a must-do bucket list activity to add in a bit of excitement and adventure into their vacation. All of these reasons are valid.

For me, it was a combination of all of these aspects. I wanted to experience the feeling of being underwater and had heard that the feeling of weightlessness was something you would not forget in a hurry. Most of all though, I was fascinated by the idea of being physically immersed in an environment that humans are not designed to be in. This idea still fills me with awe.

Although I had often thought about learning scuba diving, I didn't actually do it until I was in my mid-thirties. There are many reasons why this is. I perceived it as a very specialized activity that would be expensive to learn and undertake regularly.

When I saw the equipment involved it looked too technical, and I thought I would have trouble understanding it all. Life also has a habit of just taking over and you easily forget about such things until they pop back up on your radar further down the road.

As you'll likely discover as you read on, there are a few common misconceptions about diving. Cost is one of them. Learning to dive can be as cheap or expensive as buying a low or mid-range smartphone, depending on where you do your training and who with. Going for a dive once qualified can cost as little as $20 or as much as $300, depending on where you go.

## What does it involve, is it difficult?

SCUBA stands for Self-Contained Underwater Breathing Apparatus. This means you carry everything you need with you during a dive. Before entering the water, there are a number of steps that you need to take. You set up your equipment and test that it's working properly. You discuss what you'll do on the dive with the people you will be diving with, and undertake a "buddy check" to ensure that everyone's equipment is working as it should and that you are familiar with each other's gear.

Throughout a dive, the aim is to be as relaxed as possible and remain effortlessly at the same level in the water column by using good "buoyancy" control. You will discover quite early that understanding buoyancy and how to manipulate it is the key to becoming a good diver. Fins are used to propel you in the water with minimal effort, and your body position should be horizontal to make it easier to push through the water.

You must stay with your buddy throughout a dive and follow certain rules about how deep you can go and for how long. A dive ends when your air supply reaches a certain level, normally one-third of your supply. This is to always ensure that you have a reserve in case something unforeseen happens.

As you ascend back to the surface, you must always do so slowly because of the way that the gases you are breathing interact with your body. Divers should always be able to make a direct ascent to the surface. Diving into an overhead environment such as a wreck is very dangerous without comprehensive further training.

A diving course is all about building up the knowledge and practical ability to be able to do all of the above safely. The process of diving is no more technical or difficult for most people than driving a car. There are elements that require a solid theoretical understanding and physical actions that need to be performed. These need to be practiced and must be combined to be effective.

Being a safe diver is the overall aim of basic dive training. Under progressive supervision, diving skills and procedures become easier to perform. By the end of the course, most people are able to demonstrate that they are able to dive safely.

Using the analogy of learning to drive a car, how difficult was reverse parking during those first few driving lessons? How difficult is it now... ok bad analogy, diving won't be something that you'll actively avoid!

A newly qualified open water diver in Bali, Indonesia

## Is diving dangerous?

There are inherent risks in any activity that you do, and diving is no different. People have been scuba diving recreationally since the 1950s and in that time we've learned a lot about what can go wrong and what we can do to stay as safe as possible.

With any activity, you cannot eliminate risk completely, but what you can do is to learn how to fail safely. This is what comprehensive scuba training is all about. Individual risks are not outlined in detail in this book, that is what a scuba course is for. However, a basic description is outlined below.

The risk of injury when diving can be a difficult topic to broach with a non-diver. There is always the danger that it might scare you and put you off wanting to get trained. That said, it would be irresponsible to sugar coat- things can and do go wrong when diving and injury can occur. Such injuries include:

Decompression Sickness (DCS), commonly known as the bends- When underwater, the gases that you breath are under pressure (as is your body). They dissolve into your tissues and are released through the lungs as your ascent from depth reduces ambient pressure. DCS occurs when gas cannot be released quickly enough from your blood or tissues, which results in a bubble being formed.

DCS normally occurs because a diver has stayed too long at depth, and/or ascended too quickly from a dive. Diving procedures are designed to minimize the risk of DCS, but there is a small chance that it can still occur even when obeying all the rules. Treatment includes breathing pure oxygen and spending time in a hyperbaric chamber.

Most cases of DCS are minor and easily treatable- as long as it is treated quickly within the first few hours of symptoms appearing. Statistically, there are 10-20 cases of DCS in every 100,000 dives, which is actually very low. This is all put into context during your course.

Pulmonary barotrauma- also called an overexpansion injury. When ambient pressure is reduced, gases expand. If you hold your breath and then ascend during a dive, the air in your lungs will also expand and you can damage your lungs. So the number one rule of diving is that you should never hold your breath. I'm guessing you're pretty good at that on land. Always breath continuously and you will have no issues- providing that you are physically fit.

Marine life injury- This means being bitten or stung. You do need to stay away from things like jellyfish and give enough space between you and any fish. If you see a moray eel in a rock, and you approach it and hold your hand out, then sorry, you asked to be bitten. Most marine animals will only bite you out of self-defense as a last resort, often when physically cornered. Always observe marine life from a respectful distance.

Surface boating incidents- These include collisions with boats, and injury when on a boat. Busy diving locations will have a lot of boats on the water. Incidents of divers being hit by boats do occur. In places like North America and the UK, strict laws must be followed by boat captains when driving on and around dive sites. In places like Thailand and Indonesia, laws and common sense are sometimes flouted.

The risk of injury can be reduced by the dive operator choosing diving spots with less boat traffic. It's also essential to be vigilant when ascending to the surface from a dive. A Surface Marker Buoy (SMB) should be used by divers to warn boats that there are divers in the water.

Many people are not used to being on a boat and are often not very sure-footed. Boat decks can be very slippery and care should be taken at all times when walking around. In rougher seas, it's better to sit down and stay put until the boat has stopped.

All of the above injuries are outlined during a course, including the level of risk, symptoms, treatment, and what to do to minimize their risk of occurrence.

## Managing risk

Risk of injury applies to any hobby or activity. You don't get on a horse without knowing that you could fall off. You don't climb into a canoe without knowing that it could roll over. You don't cross the road without looking both ways.

Any discussion of potential injury has to be put into context. You can't just look at how many people break their leg when falling off a horse, you must compare it with the total number of people who ride. The same applies to diving. When considering the number of people who dive, the occurrences outlined above are rare. As mentioned already, diving courses are designed to provide you with tools to manage risk.

The vast majority of people that get injured when diving do so because they ignored what they were taught during their training, their ego took over, or they just thought they were immortal and pushed themselves beyond their comfort zone. In other words, most diving incidents occur because of bad individual and collective decision making and ignoring important safety limits taught during training.

A common saying in scuba circles is, *"there are old divers and bold divers, but there aren't many old, bold divers"*. If reading that makes little sense, then maybe diving isn't for you.

The key to staying as safe as possible is to seek good quality training and stay within well-defined limits. This book will help you to find a reputable dive center. Importantly, you need to keep on diving after your initial course, to allow you to practice and keep everything familiar.

## Sharks and diving- the reality

On a personal note, one reason that it took me so long to learn diving seems very silly now, but it was very real to me at the time and I think for a lot of people- fear of sharks. Did I really just start talking about sharks at the beginning of a book aimed at wannabe divers!? Yes. Our attitudes and perceptions of sharks are wrong. You need the right information from the very beginning.

I grew up watching Jaws, and I don't think I'm alone when I say that it left a very deep subconscious impression on me, creating some very irrational fears as I grew up. They took a long time to get over. Intentionally donning scuba gear and hanging out in a shark's environment was something I just didn't know if I could do.

My perceptions only changed when I finally went for it and did a scuba course. Everything I had previously thought was way off the mark or just plain wrong. We now know more about sharks than we ever did, and one thing is certain, they are not the mindless killers that they're often portrayed to be in the news and in movies.

Divers regularly dive with many different species of sharks, including tiger sharks and bull sharks. Divers in the USA, South Africa, Australia, and New Zealand enter the domain of the great white shark every day. Certainly, caution and good judgment should always be exercised, but incidents are generally rare.

Biologists have a better understanding of shark behavior, and importantly, how to act when around them. A sense of proportionality is required; more people are crushed by cows or killed by falling coconuts each year than are killed by sharks. In a very strange statistic, more people are also killed by slot machines falling on them.

Sadly, anyone with a serious fear of sharks is unlikely to be reading this book. Those that have some anxiety can (I hope) take comfort that it is normal to feel anxious about diving with them.

After scuba training, most people no longer have any anxiety about sharks and realize that it's actually not very common to see a shark during a dive (except in places where you intentionally go to dive with them). If you do see a shark, you will be so in awe that you won't even remember that you ever had a fear of them.

# Certification courses

## Try Dives

Without having to enroll in a certification course, it's possible to undertake a so-called "try dive". These one-day programs are designed to allow you to experience being underwater without committing to undertake a full certification program.

During a try dive, you will be introduced to diving equipment, be given basic safety information, and be coached on how to act underwater. An instructor will be with you underwater to provide assistance at all times. To participate, you need to be physically healthy and at least 10 years old. Be aware that this activity does not provide any kind of certification to dive.

There is no limit to the amount of try dive programs you can do, but if you find that you enjoyed diving and wish to do it again, it's cheaper in the long run to undertake a certification course.

## Open water and scuba diver certification

There are two courses that you can take in order to learn how to dive and become certified. You can become a **scuba diver** or an **open water diver**. The open water diver course is the primary qualification that most people sign up for. Certification will allow you to dive autonomously (without a dive professional present) to a maximum depth of 60ft (18m) with another diver- diving is not a solo sport.

The scuba diver course is a shorter program that allows you to dive to 40ft (12m), but upon certification, you must be supervised by a scuba instructor.

An open water course involves more theory and two more dives than the scuba diver course. The requirements to sign up for both courses are the same. You can enroll on the scuba diver course and then decide to continue immediately on to become an open water diver, or you can begin the open water course and stop once you fulfill the requirements for scuba diver. In this guide, we will focus only on the open water diver course.

In order to enroll in an open water or scuba diving course, you must be 15 years old, in good physical health, and be able to swim comfortably. No previous scuba diving experience is required to enroll in a course.

## Junior certification

A junior open water certification is available to children between the ages of 10 to 14 years old. The certification depth limit for 10-11-year-olds is restricted to 40ft (12m). After certification, 10-11-year-olds must dive with either a dive professional or a certified parent or guardian.

12-14-year-olds can dive to 60ft (18m), but they must dive with an adult certified diver. At the age of 15, junior open water divers can upgrade to full open water diver. This is an administrative process through the training agency, and no additional physical training is required.

## Duration

As outlined in the next chapter, the length of training depends on whether you learn full-time or part-time. A course completed in one go may take 3 to 6 days. A part-time course can take anything from 4 weeks to 6 months (in rare cases, up to a year), depending on where you live and how available you and your instructors are.

## Course content

Subjects that are covered on an open water course are outlined below. Topics covered, and certification provided is almost identical between agencies (A later chapter is dedicated to diving agencies such as PADI, SSI, BSAC, GUE, and Raid):

- Theory on physiology, physics, equipment, dive planning & procedures, and the environment.
- A pool session covering all required diving skills
- 4x open water dives (5 dives with Raid and BSAC, 6 dives with GUE)
- Certification to dive no deeper than 60ft (18m) (66ft or 20m with Raid and BSAC, 70ft or 21m with GUE)
- Certification recognized around the world
- Other agencies recognize the certification for further training

## Cost

Costs vary hugely around the world. You can pay anywhere from $300 US, all the way up to $800 US, depending on the Country. Places like Thailand and Honduras are renowned for being cheap, with courses sitting pretty steadily in the $300 US range. Countries that have a high cost of living can be much more expensive than this. If you want to learn to dive in Iceland for example, expect to pay upwards of $800 US.

The best approach is to get on Google and compare local dive shops. They shouldn't be too different from each other. If they are, then it might be worth contacting them to ask why they are so much cheaper or expensive than their competition. Ask what's included in the price to allow a better comparison.

Some diving agencies are structured as a club, which may suit your needs better than going with a commercial business. The British Sub Aqua Club offers training that is essentially free. You pay an annual membership fee and must pay for the written materials for a course. However, training is conducted on a voluntary basis by club instructors. As far as I'm aware, there are no equivalent organizations to BSAC in the US.

The downside to this approach is that you are dependent on instructors being available as they teach in a voluntary capacity in their spare time, so it can take a long time to get certified. You will also need to check whether they can provide you with dive equipment for the course, some items you will have to buy yourself.

# Course prerequisites

## Age limits

Ages requirements for open water and junior open water were outlined in more detail in the previous chapter. 10-14-year-olds may participate in the Junior open water course. The age requirement for open water is 15 years old.

It's possible for children to experience diving from the age of 8, but there are increased restrictions in terms of supervision and depth. PADI has a "bubble maker" program, and SSI has a "Scuba ranger" program. These give children the opportunity to dive in a shallow swimming pool under close supervision.

At the other end of the scale, there is no official upper age limit for diving. It depends entirely on the individual and how physically and mentally fit they feel. It should be pointed out that with increasing age, the risks of diving do increase. Older people, in general, are at a greater risk of stroke and heart attack. Divers over 40 should always seek regular medical check-ups and follow the advice of their physician.

## Medical considerations

Diving is a physical activity that subjects your body to stresses that it doesn't encounter in everyday life (you won't feel them when diving). Individuals need to be physically healthy in order to participate safely in diving. If you have a pre-existing medical condition, you may or may not be allowed to dive, depending on what it is.

A medical questionnaire must be filled out when enrolling on a diving course. This will determine whether you will be able to enroll in the course. You may require a physician's approval. In some cases, a medical condition will prevent you from being able to dive. If you are in any doubt beforehand, always consult your physician.

## Mental health and anxiety

Mental fitness to dive is as important as physical fitness. Anyone with a known mental health condition should consult a physician before enrolling on a diving course.

Mild anxiety is common among student divers. Most people are nervous about what may lie ahead when they sign up for a course. But some people may have more serious issues beyond normal nerves. This can range from a fear of fish, fear of sharks, claustrophobia, and agoraphobia. Symptoms can be mild or severe. Some people may have had bad experiences with water, such as a near-drowning incident as a child.

Such people often seek to learn diving through a desire to face these fears. Becoming a safe and qualified diver is achievable for many of them. It's recommended that if you have any of the above anxieties you communicate them clearly with your potential instructor. They will advise you on the best course of action to take.

Generally, part-time training is the most effective way to learn to dive under such circumstances. This will give you very gradual exposure and allow you to progress at a pace that you're comfortable with. It may still be possible to undertake a full-time course, but you should opt to go one-on-one with an instructor. Be aware that costs may be higher if training takes longer than a standard course.

If your anxiety is severe, then you may need to accept that diving might not be appropriate for you. The worst thing that can happen to a diver underwater is panic. Whilst panic may occur during the early stages of a course, an instructor is there to help you through the situation. But if you are prone to panic or suffer from panic attacks, diving would be too dangerous for you.

You are the person that knows how severe your anxiety is. You would need to work with your instructor to honestly assess whether you could successfully overcome your anxiety with gradual training or not.

## Swimming ability

If you're a poor swimmer and have anxiety about whether you'll be capable of achieving the requirements of an open water course, you can always test yourself to see if you can pass the swimming tests outlined later in this book. Just ensure that you have someone to look out for you, such as a lifeguard or a watchful friend who's a strong swimmer.

If you are unable to pass the swimming requirements for diving, you're advised to seek professional swimming coaching prior to enrolling on a diving course.

# Diving Agencies

When you sign up to undertake an open water course, you do so at a dive center, which is usually a commercial business. They will run the course and allocate an instructor to teach you for the duration of the program. However, the certification that you receive and program of training that the instructor will be following is provided by one of many diving agencies.

Most non-divers have heard of PADI- the Professional Association of Diving Instructors. However, just as there are many manufacturers of cars, PADI is one of over a hundred scuba diving agencies that you can be certified to dive through. They just happen to be the largest and best known.

Hearing about diving agencies other than PADI can initially be confusing to anyone interested in learning to dive, which is a testament to the success of their marketing over the years. Whilst there are some differences between how the different agencies teach you, what they teach is essentially the same. As is the qualification you will receive.

Below is a list of the most prominent worldwide dive training organizations that you are likely to encounter when seeking training. There are too many agencies to provide a full list here. You can find a complete list on Wikipedia by searching for "List of diver certification organizations".

- PADI (Professional Association of Diving Instructors)
- SSI (Scuba Schools International)
- SDI (Scuba Diving International)
- BSAC (British Sub Aqua Club)
- Raid (previously known as the Rebreather Association of International Divers)
- NAUI (National Association of Underwater Instructors)
- CMAS (Confédération Mondiale des Activités Subaquatiques)
- GUE (Global Underwater Explorers)

## The World Recreational Scuba Training Council (WRSTC)

The WRSTC was created in 1999 to create a consistent set of training standards across all diving agencies. This means that, with the exception of a few larger training agencies (notably the French agency CMAS), the skills you learn during an open water course will be largely the same whether you learn through PADI, or for example, SSI (Scuba Schools International)- the second largest scuba agency.

## Which dive agency should you choose?

Because there is so much choice when it comes to deciding whom to get certified with, making a decision can be difficult. When you approach a dive center to ask about training, they will try to persuade you to choose whatever agency that they predominantly teach. They want your business after all. But they should be honest about the consequences of choosing one agency or another, and go through the differences with you.

The reality is, each qualification is essentially the same in terms of what it allows you to do once you are certified. The greatest differences between dive agencies lie in how the course is run, i.e. the agency rules that your instructor must follow when running the course (so-called standards). They can have an effect on how smoothly your course goes, and include:

### Flexibility

Officially, PADI requires that diving skills in the pool session and open water dives should be done in a specific order, though some dive centers flout this rule out of sheer practicality. In contrast, with SSI and other agencies, the instructor is allowed to decide when to do each diving skill, as long as all skills all completed.

What this means for you- You may have trouble getting water out of your mask in the pool. This is a very common issue and it can take time to feel comfortable breathing through a regulator whilst having water around your nose. With PADI you are not allowed to continue the course until you have successfully mastered that particular skill. For anyone that is nervous, this will likely make them more nervous. Other people in the group must wait for however long it takes you to complete this skill properly. Knowing that people are waiting for you may add additional stress to the situation.

The only way forward is to either push through and get the skill done, to quit, or to temporarily pause and then continue where you left off another time, one-on-one with the instructor. This may be logistically difficult for the instructor to accommodate due to the time constraints of having to run two separate pool sessions in one day.

All other organizations provide flexibility regarding diving skills. So if you have trouble with a particular skill you can continue with the rest of the session alongside the group, and then go back to the problem skill once the session has finished- one-on-one. It's fairly obvious that this is a better approach for everyone.

## Materials

The theory part of an open water course is largely the same between all agencies, physics is physics, and physiology is physiology. There are minor differences when it comes to the theory of dive planning, as each agency uses their own set of "dive tables", but the basic set of rules for diving are mostly the same.

The main differences lie in how the information is presented to you. If you are given a physical book for the course, with PADI you own that book. With SSI, you can borrow the book and give it back at the end. This may be useful if you are traveling and don't wish to increase your baggage allowance, but it is also useful to have a reference after the course is over.

Dive agencies also allow you to complete the open water theory online via so-called "elearning". You can do this at home in your own time well before starting your actual training. There will be some recapping with your instructor, but on the whole, this approach allows more time to focus on the physical aspects of a course. With Raid, all theory must be done online.

Raid arguably has the most up to date and comprehensive materials of all the agencies. Once the course is completed, most agencies give you continued access to the elearning materials you completed.

# Proof of certification

When you want to go diving anywhere in the world, you need to show proof of your qualification. This previously meant showing your certification card. But times have changed. The card on your app will now suffice. Failing that, showing your certification email is also usually acceptable to most dive centers.

Most people have smartphones nowadays, and almost all dive centers will have wifi. If you are diving somewhere particularly remote, download your card or certification email as a PDF and save it on your phone before leaving civilization.

As PADI has always been the most widely known dive agency, people historically tended to go with what they knew. Even up to 5 years ago there was a fear amongst prospective and new divers that their SSI or SDI card would not be recognized by other dive shops, meaning they would not be allowed to dive. This is no longer the case. If you go to any dive shop in the world and they say they have never heard of SSI, SDI, BSAC or Raid, and will not acknowledge your qualification, run away, seriously- they don't know what they are doing and that does not bode well if you are trusting them to facilitate your diving!

If you are unable to show proof of your certification, a dive shop can search on the agency database to find you, as long as you give them the exact name you gave when you were certified, along with your date of birth.

Not all agencies have a database though. Dive centers can also only search for your certification if they have access to the agency database. If you are an SSI diver that wants to dive at a PADI shop and they have no affiliation with SSI, they may not be able to access the database to find your certification. The simple solution is to be prepared and ensure that one way or another you can prove your certification in one of the above ways.

A word of caution- Qualified divers often use a "logbook" to record the dives that they have done. Many are under the impression that simply showing this to a dive shop is proof of certification. It is not. It's entirely at the discretion of the dive center whether they will accept this as proof of certification or not.

## Changing agencies on future courses

Once your open water is completed, you can do your next course with a different agency. For example, if you did your open water course with PADI but then find yourself at a dive center that offers further training only with SSI, don't panic! It's really not an issue. Each agency recognizes qualifications from other agencies. As a PADI open water diver, you are eligible to enroll in an SSI advanced adventurer course, which is the next level of certification.

Your certifications are interchangeable from level to level, and between agencies. To illustrate the point, you can undertake a PADI open water course, then an SSI advanced course, then an SDI rescue course, and finally a Raid divemaster course. Or you can stick with one agency through all of your training.

# Other considerations

## Physical and digital cert cards

In a commendable effort to reduce plastic and be more environmentally responsible, the larger diving agencies are moving away from issuing physical certification cards. Certification is now stored online. You should receive an email from the agency to confirm that you've been certified. You'll then be encouraged to download the agency's app, which will display your certification.

Some agencies do still give you the option of paying extra for a physical card, but it's only a matter of time before this is phased out across all agencies.

## Referral programs

If for some reason you're unable to complete a course, most agencies have a referral program that you can use. Your instructor will fill out a referral form, which outlines how much of the course you've completed. You can then present the form to a different dive center, who will then finish your training.

Referral forms are valid for 6 months to 1 year depending on the agency, and additional costs will apply. This can be handy if you want to do the theory, exam and pool sessions locally, but then undertake the open water dives on vacation. Most agencies will accept student referrals from different organizations, but it's best to check first.

## Diving insurance

Just as most people get travel insurance when traveling abroad, it's a good idea to also get diving insurance. That doesn't mean you need to spend a fortune on an annual policy, temporary insurance for the duration of a course is both readily available and reasonably priced. It's worth checking if your travel insurance already covers you. If not, dive centers may be able to set it up for you or point you in the right direction of where to get it.

Dive Assure is a popular choice, but restrictions apply for US citizens (they only provide cover if you'll be diving outside of the US). You can get a quote from a link at the end of the book.

## Choosing an instructor

Considering the small differences between dive agencies, the main factors affecting your course will be the overall duration of training and your instructor's approach. The length of a course is outlined in the next chapter. Discussions on the suitability of an instructor could go on forever; but as this is a short guide, here are some of the more important considerations.

### Experience

In tropical locations, you are much more likely to be taught by an instructor that has less than 2 years of teaching experience. Teaching diving is popular amongst gap year students and people who wish to earn as they travel. But that doesn't at all mean that they don't know what they're doing; the upside to working as a dive professional in a tropical paradise is that you dive every day and gain teaching experience of that particular environment quickly. In colder locations, gaining teaching experience can take longer because fewer course are generally taught per week or month.

Coldwater and tropical instructors teach in very different environments. The approaches they take when teaching a course may differ, but the qualities that make a good instructor are applicable to all of them. You shouldn't dismiss an instructor because they are new to teaching. In fact, most new instructors teach with a high level of dedication and enthusiasm.

Personally, I have encountered experienced instructors that have blown me away with their sheer depth of knowledge, passion, and ability to get the best out of you. I've also met brand new instructors with drive and passion, and a desire to be the best instructor that they possibly can.

Of course, on the other side of the coin, I've come across newer instructors that care more about using their credentials to attract a mate than teaching a good course, and have also encountered some very jaded experienced instructors that deviate from agency standards because "they know best". These individuals are completely burned out and their approach is lazy. They should have found an alternative career years ago. Hopefully, with either type, you'll spot them a mile off.

### Do you pick them or they pick you?

If you've decided that you'll be learning locally, you'll have the time to shop around properly and ask a lot of questions about how the instructor teaches a course (you can find a list of questions to ask them at the end of the book).

In diving hotspots, although it's a good idea to search for prospective dive centers when booking your vacation, many people tend to arrive at their destination before deciding whom they want to dive with; particularly backpackers who decide to go somewhere at short notice. If that includes you, then you're hardly going to spend 2 or 3 days interviewing instructors with a clipboard and pen. You'll want to get cracking with the course in the limited time that you have.

Because of the way that such dive centers operate, you will be signing up for a course rather than seeking a specific instructor to teach you. Who teaches your course will depend on who's available to be allocated unless the person that greets you is the instructor that's scheduled to begin the next class (this is common). Getting a feel for the overall dive center will give you a good sense of the kind of people they have working there.

### The right instructor for you

If you do get the chance to talk to your instructor before signing up, it will help to give you a sense of how you might interact during the course. They will gladly tell you their experience and approach to teaching, and answer any questions that you may have.

The overall feeling that you'll get will depend on what you prefer in terms of teaching styles and personality traits; some things are an obvious turn off to anyone, such as arrogance. Other attributes are infectious, such as confidence, enthusiasm, and a perception that they know their craft well.

There's little point in telling you to ask them in detail how they teach buoyancy during a course, as you'll have no meaningful understanding of how to properly weigh up their answer. Instead, try to get a sense of how thorough they are, whether they seem to be sugar coating everything or appear honest about any concerns you might have, and if they come across as sincere and reliable or not.

You'll find that most instructors have the right attitude, and will be eager to ensure that you get the best experience possible.

## How good a diver will I be?

When you learn to ride a bike as a kid, there comes a point when the stabilizers are removed. It's a milestone for sure, but it really marks the point at which you are ready to go out and practice without having someone or something holding you up.

Over the duration of a 3 day open water course, there is really only enough time to get you to correctly follow the rules of diving and ensure that you can use the equipment as you should; certification means removing the stabilizers; you need to keep diving and practicing in order to truly become a "good" diver.

Being a good diver really means that you are able to stay calm and relaxed, and your ability to maintain buoyancy control can be done with little effort. It also means having a good horizontal body position (known as trim), a good level of awareness of everything that is occurring during the dive, and an ability to read the conditions to allow you to stay safe. You should always have your buddy close to you and know your air supply at all times. Crucially, a good diver is able to react calmly and appropriately, should something go wrong.

Whilst you learn the tools to achieve these in the open water course, you don't get enough time to practice them enough to become as competent as is described above. Most divers will tell you that they really started to feel comfortable and competent after around 20 dives. Everyone is different, but every dive is an opportunity to improve.

## "DIR" training

Alongside the larger dive training organizations, there are a small number of so-called "DIR" agencies that provide very high-quality dive training. Courses are longer and more thorough than with PADI, SSI, etc. DIR stands for Do It Right. The oldest and most established of these organizations is Global Underwater Explorers (GUE).

GUE was formed in 1998 by Jarrod Jablonski, a cave diver who wanted to create a standardized way of diving in order to simplify the process and increase safety. GUE training is extremely comprehensive and more demanding than training with more popular agencies. Standards and expectations are higher. On the whole, this creates more competent divers compared with divers certified under the more popular agencies.

One of the benefits of this standardized approach is that a diver trained in Okinawa could arrange to dive with a diver trained in Brazil that they have never met, and be completely familiar with their equipment and method of diving. This is not the case with agencies such as PADI or SSI, hand signals vary, buddy checks vary, and equipment really varies.

Other DIR agencies include Unified Team Diving and Inner Space Explorers. The owners of these agencies previously dived with GUE but broke away to do their own thing. Whether they knew better than GUE, or just got too big for their boots, I'll leave for another book. The training that they provide is very similar to that provided by GUE.

GUE divers getting ready for a dive at Divewise Malta

With GUE, the equivalent of an open water course is called Recreational Diver 1, or Rec 1 for short. Training is only available full-time. To enroll in a course, you must be 14 years old or older, a non-smoker, and obtain a physician's approval.

The Rec 1 course includes the following:

- Classroom work
- Land drills
- 10 aquatic (pool) sessions
- 6 open water dives
- 40 hours of instruction
- Certification to 70ft (21m)

DIR training is more expensive than other agencies, largely because the course is twice as long as a standard open water course. If you are really intent on learning to dive to a higher level than the average diver, and you like the idea of challenging yourself more, it is worth saving the money to train with an organization like GUE. In order to undertake training with any of the DIR agencies, you must contact an instructor directly, rather than through a dive center. Their website has a list of instructors local to you.

The DIR agencies are very small in comparison with PADI, SSI, BSAC, and SDI. Therefore the rest of the book will focus on standard training.

# Which method of training will suit you better?

Now that you're aware of the different dive agencies, how do you want to do your training? All in one go when on vacation? Or gradually in your spare time in evenings and weekends?

All scuba training involves theory, practical sessions in a swimming pool, and so-called "open water" dives. These can be in a lake, reservoir, pond, river, sea, or ocean. Whether you do it full-time or part-time, you will have to do all of the above. There are advantages and disadvantages to both, and it largely depends on what you want and what's convenient for you.

## Part-time courses

Part-time training is more common in northern parts of Europe, the US, and Canada. In the UK, the British Sub Aqua Club (BSAC) and Scottish Sub Aqua Club (SSAC) conduct most of their training this way.

Many diving companies provide training that is spread out over a few weeks or even months and conducted during evenings and weekends. The main advantage of learning in this way is that it is very incremental so that you don't feel overwhelmed. In each session, you will focus on learning small chunks of diving theory, or a small number of diving skills. Sessions involve practicing these skills until you are ready to progress further.

Depending on the dive center or club that you train with, schedules may be flexible. For example, if you are unable to attend a particular session, you may be able to choose alternate dates to continue where you left off. It would be wise to check whether this is possible before undertaking training, and if they have a fixed program it should really only be considered as a last resort.

When students are ready for their open water dives, be aware that the overall length of the course may depend on the weather conditions, especially if the dives will be in the ocean. Planned dives may be canceled at the last minute due to unfavorable weather, namely wind, and waves.

## Cost

Dive training costs may vary depending on whether you go with a club such as BSAC, or a commercial dive center. The overall cost of a course with a dive center should not be much different from the cost of full-time training. However, there may be added costs such as boat fees, swimming pool entrance fees, and tank fills to consider.

## Water temperatures

Open water temperatures vary, a lot. If you live in Europe or North America, temperatures may be as low as 36°F in winter (2°C), and up to 82°F in the summer (28°C). If you live in the Mediterranean, lucky you, at the height of summer the ocean is 82°F (28°C). In the winter it only drops to 60°F (16°C). In the UK the ocean might be 60°F in the summer and 43°F in the winter (6°C). In Northern Canada and Northern parts of Scandinavia, you can expect 32-43°F in the winter (0 to 6°C), and 54°F in the summer (12°C).

Any diving activity requires that you use adequate exposure protection in the form of a wetsuit or drysuit. Things can get a bit chilly, particularly towards the end of a dive. This can also make things interesting when dressing into your exposure suit. For some people, being immersed in anything other than tropical water is utterly unappealing and just not an option. If you're one of those people, it doesn't mean that diving is not for you, it simply means that you will only dive when on vacation.

If that's the case, then you may wish to take advantage of the referral system by doing the theory and pool sessions locally in your own time, and then completing the open water dives when on vacation.

Cold water doesn't necessarily mean that you will be cold, however. Drysuit diving can be very comfortable, with the added bonus that you won't even get wet (in theory).

### Advantages of part-time training

- You can progress at a pace you are comfortable with.
- You will not feel rushed
- The amount of new things to learn in each session is more manageable
- You will get more practice of each diving technique
- You will be more likely to remember what you learned in the longer term
- You can undertake some of the course nearby, and then finish it when on vacation.

### Disadvantages of part-time training

- Certification can take a long time and progress can feel slow
- It is frustrating when dives are called off
- The time between training sessions can be frustratingly long
- Diving in colder water doesn't appeal to everyone

The author, working at Silfra Fissure in Iceland. Water temperature 36°F (2°C)

## Full-time courses

Though many dive centers in temperate countries do offer full-time courses, tropical resorts are where the vast majority of people learn to dive. Notable locations include the Caribbean, Mexico, Thailand, Indonesia, the Maldives, Fiji, and many other Pacific Islands.

Open water courses are usually run over 3 days, and as with learning part-time, courses include theory, a pool session, and open water dives.

Compared with the weather conditions and water temperatures in temperate climates, what's not to love- warm tropical water, generally calm conditions, good underwater visibility, an abundance of marine life, classroom on the beach... However, you should try and avoid making direct comparisons. As outlined, there are pros and cons to each method, and you need to think long term about what your overall objectives are before, dare I say it.... diving in.

Some tropical locations are renowned for being the place to go for young travelers to get their diving license (Thailand, Indonesia, Mexico). Courses are cheap and diving is relatively easy. I did my initial open water training in Thailand, and it was absolutely fantastic, though I did luck out with choosing a very reputable dive center (Big Blue Diving in case you were wondering).

As with anything else, there are reputable operators and not so reputable operators, These Countries have lower regulatory requirements compared with North America and Europe. Many operators take advantage of that fact. Standards of training can vary wildly as a result.

## Advice on choosing a dive center

The main disadvantage of prospective divers is that they don't know what they don't know. How do you know what to look out for if you don't know how things are supposed to be? The information here will help you to choose the right kind of dive operator for you. I strongly recommend that you do your research before committing to undertake a course. Here are a few things to be aware of.

### Cost

Cheap doesn't always mean better. In fact, it can be a good indicator of which specific dive centers to avoid. Remember though that prices in Asian and South American Countries will inevitably be cheaper than in North America and Europe.

You may be on a very limited budget but think long term. You get what you pay for. Competition for new students in popular dive spots can be incredibly high, leading to discounts that are often too good to be true. In such cases, operating costs are kept to the absolute bare minimum, and this often translates into bargain basement training. Think budget airlines, but without the chargeable extras being available.

With distinctly undercut prices, you may not realize that corners are being cut, but they often are. Whether that means saving money on diesel by taking you to the same nearby dive site for all your dives, trying to get the course done faster than 3 days, paying their staff terrible wages (and killing their motivation), or cramming as many students as they can into a course, they all diminish the experience that you should be getting.

It's impossible to put a minimum price on courses, but as an example, in Bali, Indonesia, the average cost of an open water course is $300-$350 US. However, a small number of dive centers are offering courses at $220 US (at the time of printing). It's no surprise that theses dive centers are renowned within the industry for offering poor quality training.

If there's one thing to remember here, it's this- The most reputable companies will resist reducing their prices, as they know that it will impact their ability to provide good training. Here are a few things to investigate before signing up for a course:

## Equipment

If equipment looks torn and tattered, it's pretty obvious that they are not spending the money to maintain it correctly. Scuba gear is life support equipment, and regular maintenance is not something that should be neglected. Don't interpret this as a sure-fire sign that your safety is being compromised. If anything goes wrong with your equipment your instructor will be right there to deal with it. It's more of an indication that the dive center is not providing what they should be.

Ask to see their equipment before committing to sign up for training. There will always be wear and tear, especially in a busy dive center, and you need to accept that not all gear will be brand new and shiny. But when all of their equipment looks badly worn, it will be pretty obvious and is not a good sign. A reputable dive center knows this, and they will be happy to show you their wares. A not so reputable outfit will wheel out all kinds of excuses and distractions.

Of course, all this is easy for me to say. At this stage, you don't even know what equipment is used for diving! Look for wetsuits that are badly ripped and tattered, and any equipment that looks very old, bleached by the sun or appears to be reliant on masking tape or cable ties to keep it together.

## Group size

The maximum amount of students allowed for each instructor is 8 to 1. That doesn't mean 8 to 1 is ok though. You will get much more out of your training if your group is small. It can be nice to be jumbled in with other people and the atmosphere of a course may be better with a slightly larger group. But the amount of individual instruction you'll get will be lower.

Also, be aware that some very busy dive centers will teach groups of up to 15 people at a time. They get away with this by having certified assistants sitting in on the course. This means new instructors or divemasters, who are often only there to enable a larger instructor to student ratio.

Given the above, how effective do you think the individual tuition will be with a group of this size when the course is run in the same amount of time? Ask the dive center what their maximum group size is. If it's more than 4, ask to be put into a smaller group or consider going elsewhere.

## The overall feel of the dive center

Sometimes when you walk into a shop you can immediately sense that something's not right; staff are not friendly and it just feels impersonal or chaotic. Diving is no different. If you get the chance, hang around the shop and talk to the staff before signing up. You'll be able to gauge whether it fits in with what you are looking for; if it's laid back, too laid back, bustling with activity or just absolute chaos. Obviously, there's not much point in entering a large busy dive center if you're looking for a small outfit with a more personalized approach.

## Your instructor

If you get the chance, talk to your potential instructor before signing up. Most instructors are professional, knowledgeable and passionate about teaching diving. If you have any anxiety about diving, bring it up with them, they've heard it before and are very good at allaying pre-course fears.

Do be on the lookout for the occasional instructor that is more interested in living a tropical lifestyle than imparting their passion and knowledge of diving. They are thankfully in the minority and are relatively easy to spot.

The training they will provide will not be as comprehensive as you deserve.

Dive centers that appear to only focus on the coolness of their brand should be avoided at all costs. They attract staff who consider being associated with the brand more important than building a good reputation for comprehensive and safe training. Dedication to learning their craft is often low on their list of priorities.

## Advantages of full-time training

- Continuous exposure can help you to absorb and embed things better. You may be surprised by how much you can learn over such a short period of time
- You'll have the rest of your vacation to go out and enjoy diving once you've completed the course
- You will meet like-minded people with similar goals to you
- The learning environment is pretty nice!

## Disadvantages of full-time training

- Quality of training can be very variable. Sometimes it is difficult to realize this until after you've already started the course, or after you've finished
- The learning curve can be steep. For some people, it's too much
- If you suffer from any kind of anxiety, you may need more time to progress gradually at a comfortable pace. Part-time training may suit you better
- Training will not be as comprehensive as in cold water environments given the time constraints imposed on instructors
- Training will not prepare you for diving in cold water

# Course content and schedule

Open water courses are comprised of an orientation, theory sessions (including a written exam), one or more pool sessions, and 4 or 5 open water dives. The exact order of each activity is decided by the dive center, based around how they organize their daily operations. In tropical locations, you may begin the course with some theory or jump straight into the pool. Part-time training normally begins with theory.

Courses are based on gradual exposure. In other words, on the first day of your course, you will not be plunged straight into the open ocean. That would be a sure fire way to get 100% of all students to drop out immediately! Instead, you'll be happy to hear that in water work begins in a pool that is around 4-5ft deep (1-1.5m).

As you make progress in the pool you'll move on to the deep end, which is usually around 10ft (3m) deep. By the end of the pool session (or sessions), you should be more than ready to apply what you have learned in open water.

The term "open water" is also a little misleading. Your first couple of dives will be sheltered dive sites close to shore, such as a bay. The first 2 dives will be no deeper than 40ft (12m), with an average depth during the dives of around 20ft (6m). Only once you've got to grips with how to dive will you go a little bit deeper on the last few dives- no deeper than 60ft (18m).

## Orientation

The very first thing you will do on any open water course is to sit down with your instructor, who will talk you through the schedule for the course. They'll tell you what to bring, when and where to meet, and outline what you'll do at each stage, including expectations of when the course is scheduled to end. This will allow you to plan your onward travel if you are on a tight vacation schedule.

You will also watch some videos about diving. These are split into the 5 sections of theory. You may watch them all in one go, or fit them in between the theory and the pool session(s).

## Liability release and medical forms

During the orientation, some paperwork needs to be filled in. This includes a liability release and a medical form. The liability release is a legal document, which will be explained to you. You are advised to read it before signing. It states that you have a responsibility during the course to act appropriately at all times. Furthermore, the instructor and dive center also have a duty of care towards you. They must act in the interest of your safety at all times.

There are inherent risks involved in diving, and your signature means that you agree to accept those risks as long as the instructor and dive center are doing everything they can to ensure your safety. You cannot undertake the course without signing it.

The WRSTC medical form is there to ensure that you don't have any pre-existing conditions that may not be safe for diving. Read it carefully and answer it honestly. It consists of questions that require a YES or NO answer. If you tick YES to any of the questions you will need to consult a doctor, who will then decide whether to sign you off as ok to dive.

A word of warning, do not lie about anything on the medical form. If you do, you are not only putting yourself at risk but also those that are diving with you. Answering YES to a question may not seem like a big deal to you, but there may be consequences underwater that you are not aware of.

For example, when someone states on the medical form that they have asthma, they are often annoyed when told that they must seek medical approval in order to be able to dive. However, should they have an asthma attack underwater, the cold, dry air coming from the scuba cylinder may make their symptoms worse. If their airway becomes restricted this can be very dangerous, for reasons you will learn in the physiology section of the theory. Some types of asthma will still allow you to dive, but you need to check with a doctor first.

Don't try and change your mind about a YES answer either. If you cross out a YES and change it to a NO, you will not be allowed to initial the change (as with legal documents) or simply fill in a new form, you must visit a physician. The instructor's duty of care is a legal requirement for them to follow procedures correctly.

If you're reading this and thinking "I'll just write NO even though my hayfever would be a YES", then you need to understand that you may be putting yourself and others at risk. If it's discovered during a course that you have a condition that you tried to cover up, you will be ejected from the course with no refund. A conscientious dive center will also warn nearby dive centers about you, to prevent you from enrolling with them without disclosing the issue.

If you are unsure about a medical condition that you may have, contact the dive center and they will send you a copy of the medical form, which you can take to a physician if necessary- well before your course starts. Remember to bring it with you to the dive center!


## Expectation management

Before starting the course, your instructor needs to explain that, just because you have signed up for the course, there are no guarantees that you will be certified at the end of it. Simply turning up is not enough. You must demonstrate that you are competent and safe. This includes your attitude, and your instructor has the final say.

Learning to dive follows a step-by-step process. Diving techniques are discussed and then demonstrated to you in the water. You will then get to practice them until you're able to do perform them competently. Everyone is different, some people have no problems at all and pick diving up with ease, others may struggle with some aspects. A small number of people find it very challenging.

Instructors are paid to coach you through any steps you are having difficulty with, and are experienced in getting the best out of you. More often than not you will just need more time to practice. This may come at an additional cost.

However, there is always the chance that things are just too challenging for you, or moving you too far out of your comfort zone too quickly. This could be because of the steep learning curve involved with only 3 days of training, or maybe you are also struggling with some form of anxiety.

Remember the duty of care that the instructor has? It would be very irresponsible of them to certify you to dive if you are not actually capable of diving properly. It might not sound like it at the time, but it's completely in your best interest to not be certified under these circumstances. It's better that you know where you stand before you begin training.

Also be aware that if you drop out of your course, you should have already discussed with the dive center what their policy is regarding refunds. You may receive a partial refund or no refund at all.

## Dive theory

The theory section of a course includes everything you need to know to be able to dive safely, including:

- Physiology- you will learn about how diving affects the air spaces in your body- sinuses, ears, lungs, and the airspace in your mask. You will need to manage these air spaces when diving. You will also be taught about potential diving injuries, their causes, symptoms, prevention, and treatment.

- Physics- Things are a little different underwater, objects appear closer than they are, sound travels faster and you can't tell where it's coming from, air is compressed so you breath more gas than on the surface, and light is absorbed by the water. An understanding of how gas behaves under pressure is fundamental to managing buoyancy.

- Diving equipment- The only reason you are able to go underwater is because of the equipment you are using. You will learn how it works, how to set it up, how to operate it when diving, and how to care for it.

- Dive planning and procedures- Amongst other things, you will learn all about dive planning, how you should move your body when underwater, how you should dive when encountering a current, how divers communicate underwater, and how you should position yourself in relation to the divers you are with. Emergency procedures are also covered.

- The environment- Winds, tides, and currents vary, depending on the location. An understanding of how they affect a dive is critical. Likewise, you are entering an alien environment, you need to learn some important "housekeeping". In other words, how you should interact with delicate ecosystems and marine life.

### Exams and homework

If you haven't gone down the route of elearning, you will need to answer some questions at the end of each chapter of your book. You will also have to sit for an exam. It's multiple choice and as long as you've gone through the book and listened to your instructor, you shouldn't have any problems. If you fail the exam, you'll be able to sit a different exam after some additional coaching.

Once the theory and exam are done, training is all hands on practical work in the water.

## Equipment set up

Before moving on to the pool session, your instructor with introduce you to the equipment. This is usually done by the side of the pool. They will explain what each item is and how it works. They will then set up their own equipment and talk you through it as you watch. Then it's your turn to set up the equipment you were allocated. The instructor will watch you do it and guide you if you get it wrong. You'll practice taking it apart and setting it up many times during the course. Diving equipment includes:

- BC- Buoyancy compensator- (PADI calls it a BCD- Buoyancy Control Device). This is the jacket that you wear. It holds the scuba cylinder on your back and allows you to change your buoyancy by adding and removing air into and out of the jacket.

- Regulator- This connects to the scuba cylinder, and reduces the high-pressure air to an intermediate pressure that you can breathe. There is a secondary hose called an "octopus" or "alternate air source", that acts as a backup and allows 2 people to breathe from one tank in an emergency. It also has an air gauge so you can see how much air is in the tank, and a hose to connect to the BC and drysuit, if applicable.

- Mask and snorkel- Not only do you need to be able to see underwater, but you also need to have a nose pocket so that you can remove any water from the mask when underwater. This is one reason why divers don't wear swimming goggles. Removing water is achieved by adding air into the mask via your nose when exhaling, and is one of the skills that you will practice during the course. The snorkel allows you to breathe comfortably on the surface without wasting the air in your cylinder.

- Wetsuit- You lose body heat 25 times faster in water than in air. The longer you are in the water, the more heat you will lose. Feeling comfortable is an important part of diving. In tropical locations, you will likely be given a 3mm thick short-sleeved, short-legged wetsuit. These are not the most fashionable of items, but they do their job. In places like Indonesia where water temperatures can be slightly cooler, you will be given a slightly thicker 5mm full-length wetsuit. In the summer in the UK, you may wear a 7mm wetsuit.

- Drysuit- In locations with colder water, it's generally recommended that you wear a drysuit. What's considered cold varies from person to person. But as a rule of thumb, temperatures below 60°F (16°C. Provided that it doesn't leak, a drysuit is designed to keep you dry during your dive. This will also keep you warmer. Drysuits have a valve that allows you to inject air from the air cylinder into the suit. This is because the suit crushes onto your body as you descend deeper underwater. The air will counteract the "squeeze". However, on the ascent, you need to vent the air as it expands due to the reduced water pressure. This is done through a valve on the upper arm or wrist.

- Wetsuit boots- These are essentially shoes that you wear, not so much to keep your feet warm, but to protect your feet from rubbing on the fins or being cut on rocks when entering the water from the shore.

- Fins- These are the things that allow you to move through the water with ease. There are many different types. In tropical spots "closed-heel" fins are very common. The foot sits in a rubber-lined opening, which can rub your feet. It's recommended to wear wetsuit socks with these. The other option is "open-heeled" fins. These have a strap that tightens around the back of your foot, which is more secure than with closed-heel fins.

- Weight belt or integrate weights- You need to wear some lead to weigh you down. This is to counteract the buoyancy of your exposure suit, your equipment, and your body's own buoyancy characteristics. Weight Belts are worn around the waist and are more commonly used. Integrated weights include pockets that fit into the BC. They are more expensive and therefore rarer for dive centers to use.

## Pool session

Pool sessions are called "confined" sessions by dive professionals. They can either take place in a swimming pool, or in a body of water that has pool-like conditions. This may be in a sheltered bay or a lake. The pool session is split into two parts, shallow and deep. You start the session in the shallow end. In topical locations, you will probably do the entire pool session in one go. With part-time training, you'll undertake several sessions.

## Swim tests

Before getting into your equipment you will need to undertake a "swim test". This is to demonstrate that you are a comfortable swimmer, able to look after yourself in the water. It's comprised of two parts:

- 10-minute float- You must tread water or float for 10 minutes in water that is too deep to stand in, without touching the sides.

- 656ft (200m) swim- You need to swim continuously for 200m, which will be numerous laps of a swimming pool. You can swim as fast or slow as you are comfortable with, and use any style you wish. Alternatively, you can use a mask, snorkel, and fins to continuously swim 984ft (300m).

For the swims, you can use an exposure suit such as a rash guard or wetsuit, but weight must be added to account for the buoyancy it provides.


## Gearing up and buddy checks

Once the swim tests are done you will be ready to get into your equipment. An important pre-dive safety check will be introduced at this point, called a buddy check. This is where you team up with another diver (your buddy) and test that your equipment is working properly. This process also familiarises you with your buddy's equipment. Each agency has its own way of doing the check.

An acronym is often used to help remember each step. Some instructors go further and turn it into a mnemonic:

PADI uses BWRAF:

B- BC
W- Weights
R- Releases
A- Air
F- Final ok.

BSAC uses BAR:

B- Buoyancy
A- Air
R- Regulator and releases

Raid uses BRAID:

B- Buoyancy
R- Regulator and releases
A- Air
I- Instruments
D- Diver ok to dive

An example of a mnemonic would be, "Barry White Records Are Funky", or "Burger With Relish and Fries". As you can imagine, more colorful variations are also used.

## Entering the pool

You will start out in the shallow section of the pool. It's not normal for a person to find themselves breathing underwater, so the first thing you need to do is to get used breathing from a regulator. A common way to do this is to get you to stay on the surface, put the regulator in your mouth and put your face in the water whilst breathing normally. You may be surprised by the noise initially as the exhalation bubbles are expelled from the regulator via an exhaust. You may then repeat without a mask.

The next step will be to show you how the BC works. Positive buoyancy is when the BC is full of air. This allows you to stay on the surface without kicking or getting tired. To get underwater, you need to become negatively buoyancy. You let air out of the BC and allow yourself to gradually sink.

Once your group is underwater, you will spend some time getting used to breathing with the regulator, and just being underwater.

## Diving skills

Before practicing any skill, the instructor will explain what the skill is, why it is necessary, and outline the steps you need to take to perform it. This will include things not to do during the skill. They will then demonstrate the skill to you underwater.

Instructors will have their own way of conducting the session. Buoyancy should be an initial first thing to practice and think about, but in busy dive centers in the tropics, time constraints, large group sizes, and small pools often prevent any kind of meaningful practice from taking place. You may go straight into learning some of the diving skills.

Below is a list of skills that you will do. The list is not exhaustive, and it is not in any particular order. It will vary between what PADI dictates, and the flexibility that instructors have with other agencies.

The range of skills that will be introduced and practiced include:

- Clearing the regulator- taking the regulator out of your mouth, replacing it, and purging the mouthpiece of water before taking a breath.
- Buoyancy- thinking about and practicing "neutral" buoyancy
- Regulator recovery- if the regulator comes out of your mouth, steps on how to find it and put it back in.
- Partially flooded mask- how to remove water from the mask
- Fully flooded mask- same process as above, but with a mask full of water
- Mask removal and replacement- flooding the mask, taking it off, replacing it and clearing it of water
- "Out of air"- an emergency procedure if someone is low or out of air
- Air depletion- a simulation of what it feels like when there's no air left in the tank.
- Free-flowing regulator- how to breathe from a regulator if it malfunctions

Once you've practiced some skills in shallow water, you'll move on to repeat them and practice new ones in deeper water. These include:

- Propulsion- different kicking techniques
- Buoyancy- swimming around and further practice
- Mask removal and replacement- repeated from the shallow end
- No mask swim- swimming without a mask on to demonstrate comfort.
- Out of air swim- sharing air and swimming horizontally as a buddy team
- Air depletion and out of air ascent- simulation of running out of air, followed by an emergency air sharing exercise to the surface
- Fin pivot- A neutral buoyancy exercise.
- Neutral buoyancy- practicing hovering at the same depth in the water column
- Weight belt removal- taking off the weight belt and replacing it underwater
- Scuba unit removal and replacement- again, done underwater
- CESA (Controlled Emergency Swimming Ascent)- simulating an emergency ascent when your buddy is not available to share air. Agencies other than PADI call this an ESA (Emergency Swimming Ascent).
- EBA (Emergency Buoyant Ascent)- similar to the CESA, but includes removing the weight belt before ascending.

## Surface skills

Some skills are done on the surface. These include:

- Water entry and exit methods
- Weight check- assessing how much weight you need to wear
- Weight drop- removing your weights to simulate an emergency
- Weight belt removal and replacement
- Scuba unit removal and replacement
- Oral inflation- inflating the BC manually
- Tired diver tow- methods for pushing and pulling a tired diver
- Cramp removal- removing cramp on yourself or a buddy
- Snorkel to regulator exchange
- DSMB deployment- filling a high visibility marker tube with air
- Snorkeling skills

Completion of each skill should be followed by a short review of how it went. Once the pool session is over you should receive a debrief, in which your performance is discussed and suggestions for improvement are made going forward.

### Kneeling down or "neutrally buoyant"?

Taking the dive industry as a whole, most divers are taught skills when kneeling down on the bottom, in the pool, and in open water. The idea behind this is that it gives the student less to think about so they can focus on learning the skill. It's the way that things have always been done.

However, this is slowly changing, and this method is increasingly being seen as a lazy way of teaching, and not at all beneficial for the student. If students kneel down a lot when training, they are not practicing buoyancy, which is the single most important aspect of diving that they need to become good at.

Furthermore, if kneeling down becomes an ingrained habit, this goes against how you should act and interact with the environment when diving in open water. Many divers damage coral and bump into things due to poor buoyancy control and lack of consideration for the environment around them.

Challenging students to think about neutral buoyancy from the very beginning of a pool session will make them better divers in a very short space of time.

When learning part-time, there is really no reason why you should be kneeling down at any point during your course. Instructors that say there is nothing wrong with kneeling down are part of the "old school" way of doing things, and this approach hinders your development as a diver. Of all instructors, they have the time to spend on developing neutral buoyancy from an early stage.

Bear in mind that in busy tropical dive centers, the instructor simply will not have the time to ingrain neutral buoyancy into a group of 4 or 6 divers during a pool session, This will mean that you will have less time overall to develop and master buoyancy control. This is in stark contrast to what some of the agencies will have you believe you can achieve over 3 days.

## Open water dives

After the theory and pool session, you are ready to take your first steps in open water. Four or five dives must be completed, depending on the agency. During each dive, you will need to repeat some of the skills practiced in the pool. The only skill that will be slightly different is the CESA with PADI. In the pool, it is practiced horizontally underwater. In the open water, it must be done vertically to the surface.

The number of skills that you do on each dive will depend on the agency and instructor's discretion, and environmental conditions. With the exception of a PADI and Raid course, instructors may decide which skills to do on each dive. They may choose to spread the skills out evenly over all four dives. Some instructors prefer to include more skills on the first two dives so that the last two dives are more about practicing buoyancy and enjoying the dive.

### Briefings

Before each dive, your instructor will give you a briefing to outline what you will be doing on the dive, and what you need to think about and work on to improve your own diving. Briefings should include the following:

- Entry and exit procedures
- Maximum depth
- Route of the dive
- Outline of skills to be conducted
- Hand signals for communication
- How each person should position themselves
- Information about the dive site
- Environmental conditions, currents, waves, etc
- Missing diver procedure
- Emergency procedures

### Getting to the dive site

Dives may be done from the shore, or from a boat. If boat diving, you may be diving from a Rigid Inflatable Boat (RIB) or Zodiac, or it may be a large purpose-built diving vessel. When diving from a RIB you will set your equipment up on land and get fully kitted up, ready to roll back into the water when arriving at the dive site.

If diving from a larger boat, you will probably set up your equipment on-route to the dive site. On arrival, you will get into your equipment, do a buddy check, and jump in the water, usually by taking a big step forward, known as the giant stride.

### In water

All dives provide an opportunity to put into practice the theory that you've learned. You will have much more space than in the pool to get a better handle on buoyancy control and how to move through the water.

As with the pool, your first two dives will be relatively shallow- no deeper than 12m. How long a dive will last is difficult to gauge, everyone breathes at a different rate, large men will use much more air than small women, but they will have the same amount of air on their back at the beginning of the dive. Add on top of this that you will be concentrating quite hard, which tends to increase your breathing rate. Your first two dives may be as short as 20 minutes or as long as an hour. A dive is ended when the first person in the group has a predetermined amount of air left in their tank.

Dives 3 and 4 are a little bit deeper but no deeper than 60ft (18m). By then you will be wearing the right amount of weight, which is continually assessed by your instructor. Too much weight affects your air consumption and diving position, too little means you will have trouble getting underwater. The more appropriately you are weighted, the easier you will find buoyancy control. This will make you more relaxed and comfortable throughout the dive. Dives 3 and especially dive 4 will likely be longer than the previous two dives, but there are no guarantees.

### Debriefs

After each dive, your instructor will debrief you on how the dives went. This should include a recap of how the skills were performed, and tips for improvement for the next dive. This is your opportunity to ask questions and have a discussion to really get the most out of your coaching.

The instructor will also show you how to log your dives. Logbooks are a useful way of keeping track of where you've been diving, how many dives you've done, and what you did on each dive, including the maximum depth and total dive time. They aren't mandatory once you're qualified, but they can be a nice reminder of the things you've done and places you've visited.

Open water divers exploring on dive 4 of their open water course, Bali, Indonesia

# Certification and future options

That's it, once you've completed the debrief for your final dive, and as long as all the exams and skills have been completed to the instructor's satisfaction, congratulations, you are now a qualified open water diver!

As part of your final debrief there will be paperwork to sign, which is you agreeing that all aspects of the course were taught correctly within agency standards. Then your instructor should go through a few things with you, such as:

## What your certification means

I don't really want to spoil the celebration, but there is some fine print involved in becoming an open water diver. When it says that you're certified to dive, there is a caveat to that. You should only dive in places with similar conditions to those that you trained in. Diving conditions can be changeable, and some places are known for having strong currents and big waves.

For example, after completing an open water course in Bonaire, Truk Lagoon, or the east coast of Thailand (places known for having calm conditions), you would find conditions in places like Komodo in Indonesia to be overwhelming. Komodo is renowned for having some of the strongest currents in the world. It would be sensible to gain more experience in easier conditions before you feel comfortable to dive such places.

Remember also that you should never dive alone. The entire system of safety centers around using a "buddy system".

## Extended periods without diving

Although your certification is technically valid for life, if you don't dive for a long time you'll need to undertake a refresher course. This is a one day program where you will go through some skills and undertake a shallow dive with a divemaster or instructor to get you back into the swing of things.

There's no fixed time period of what's considered too long an absence from diving, it's at the discretion of the dive center you want to dive with. It's normally 12 months, but it could be as little as 6 months or as great as

18 months. It also depends on how many dives you've done overall. If it's more than 100, then they may be a little more relaxed and a check out dive will usually suffice.

Check-out dives are often required by dive centers. These are shallow dives that allow a dive center to stealthily see how competent you are in the water. They are not doing this to judge you, they just want to group you with other divers that have similar experience and air consumption, so you get the most out of your dive. Check-out dives also enable you to ensure that your equipment is working properly and your weighting is correct.

Always be cautious if you haven't dived in a while. Talk to dive staff, and don't be annoyed if they tell you that you need a refresher; they're acting in your best interest. If you do 4 dives on an open water course and then don't dive again for 6 months, how much do you honestly think you will remember from your course?

## Gaining experience safely

Although there is nothing technically stopping you from buying some scuba equipment and going for a dive with a buddy, the majority of new divers sensibly prefer to gain experience under the supervision and care of a dive center. Remember that your qualification is only valid in similar conditions to those that you learned to dive in. Unfamiliar locations may be hazardous without gaining local knowledge and initial supervision.

## Making the transition to cold-water diving

If you learned to dive in a tropical location, you will not be prepared for diving in cold water. The use of a drysuit requires further training, and conditions may be very different from a warm coral reef with good underwater visibility. These can quickly become overwhelming for a new diver.

Water in places like the UK or northeast coast of the US can be green, murky, and choppy. Underwater visibility may be as little as 3 feet (1m). This is not for everyone, but there is a lot of incredible marine life in these kinds of conditions. Contact a local dive center and they will help you to make the transition safely.

## What's next?

The possibilities are endless. But generally, you need to just go diving. You'll be surprised by just how much you improve after only another 5-10 dives. Once you've done 50 dives it's a safe bet that you're in it for the long haul.

The next step in terms of certification is an advanced open water course (SSI calls it Advanced Adventurer). This consists of 5 "themed" dives to give you a taste of different types of diving. You will learn some basic navigation techniques, potentially dive a wreck, night dive, and learn to dive to 100ft (30m). This does open up a lot more dives sites around the world to you.

There are a host of so-called "speciality" courses that you could do based on your interests. This ranges from wreck diver, shark diver, or drift diver (diving in currents). To be completely honest, most of them are a complete waste of your time and are just a way for dive agencies to get more money out of you. Just go diving.

The exception to this rule is a nitrox course. Nitrox is a gas mixture containing more oxygen. There are benefits to using it, but also hazards that are outlined on a course. A wreck course can also be very useful, provided that you train with an instructor that is also a technical dive instructor with experience and skills in this type of diving. Although most dive instructors may be qualified to teach it on paper, if they haven't received proper training themselves, they will have no idea how to teach it properly.

Once you've completed your advanced course and gained more experience, the next step in the ladder of training is to become a rescue diver. To enroll in this course you need to have an emergency first response qualification, which is a non-diving course that you can also take at a dive center.

The rescue course emphasizes helping other divers, including tired or panicking divers, and surfacing unconscious divers. It also covers the procedures that are required to manage an emergency situation. It's the first step towards becoming a professional diver but is a valuable undertaking even if you only decide to dive for fun.

## Taking the advanced course straight away

Throughout your open water course, your instructor may subtly encourage you to undertake the advanced course immediately afterward. They often have a financial incentive for doing so, but that doesn't mean that they are only looking out for themselves. Of all people that learn to dive, 90% of them will never dive again after completing their course; it was only ever a bucket list item to tick off. In contrast, those who undertake the advanced course are much more likely to continue diving, further down the road.

Whilst there can be benefits to jumping straight into the advanced course, you need to make an honest assessment of how well you think you picked everything up during the open water course. If you weren't capable of diving, you shouldn't have been certified. But you may feel that you need to continue diving at the same level to get more practice and consolidate everything that you learned. This is a sensible approach. You'll get more out of the advanced course later on, as your brain won't need to focus so much on the basics.

On the other hand, if learning to dive was not much of a challenge and you feel that you picked everything up easily, there's really no reason not to go for it as long as you're fully aware of what's ahead. Just don't do it purely because it allows you to go deeper. Use it as a chance to get more coaching from a professional.

## Other types of diving

You may find that in time you wish to expand your horizons to try other forms of diving. There are numerous options that you can choose:

### Freediving

Freediving involves exploring underwater on a single breath. It requires little equipment compared with scuba diving and is becoming more and more popular. Many people are attracted to the freedom it affords, and inner mental focus that is required to undertake it.

As with scuba diving, it is essential to seek properly sanctioned training through agencies such as PADI, SSI, Raid, and AIDA (Association Internationale pour le Développement de l'Apnée). Dive centers are increasingly branching out to offer freediving training.

Be aware that there are individuals and "organizations" that offer freediver training that is known to include dangerous practices. They do not provide proper certifications from any of the above agencies, and they should be avoided at all costs. Be wary of such training in the Philippines in particular. The only way to ensure that you will receive proper instruction is to get certified through one of the above agencies.

## Technical Diving

Technical diving is an advanced form of scuba diving that requires additional training. During open water training, you are taught to stay with some well-defined limits. With technical diving, you learn how to intentionally break those limits in a controlled way.

Technical diving may involve diving deeper or staying underwater for longer, or both. It also includes advanced wreck diving, cave diving, and ice diving. Mine diving is also becoming more popular, as is rebreather diving.

The author undertaking a decompression stop after a deep dive

Numerous diving agencies teach technical diving, including GUE (Global Underwater Explorers), TDI (Technical Diving International), PADI, SSI, and IANTD (International Association of Nitrox and Technical Divers).

## Underwater photography and videography

This can be a hobby in and of itself, and the options are endless in terms of how far you want to take things. You can buy modestly priced cameras with underwater housings and either teach yourself or undertake a course with a professional photographer or videographer. Some divers specialize in "macro" photography, which is close up shots of smaller creatures. Others prefer to film large pelagics such as whale sharks and manta rays.

Before even thinking about picking up a camera, you need to become very competent with your diving. Good buoyancy control is essential. If you start too early you will find that diving properly and operating the camera will be just too much for you. Your shots will also not be the masterpieces you were hoping for.

Contact a dive center to find out if they offer underwater photography training, but look beyond the standard speciality course. You can also search online for professional underwater photographers that offer training.

## What are you waiting for?

I hope that you now have a much better idea of what learning to dive is all about. For many people, the hardest part is getting around to signing up for a course. After training, most divers will tell you that they wished they'd learned to dive years ago and not left it so long to get involved. Don't be one of them!

Good luck with your training and see you for a dive sometime.

If you found this book useful, please consider leaving a short review on Amazon.

# Questions to ask an instructor and dive center

## Instructor questions

- How did you get involved in diving and teaching?
- How long have you been diving?
- How long have you been teaching?
- What kind of diving do you do for fun?
- What's your least favorite part of a course?
- What do you enjoy most about teaching?
- What's the most challenging thing about teaching?
- What's the hardest part of a course for most people?
- How soon do you start to teach buoyancy in the pool?
- Do you teach students when kneeling down?
- How often do you fail people?
- What's your approach to safety?
- What is your teaching style?
- What's your weakest area when it comes to teaching diving?
- What's your opinion of DIR training?

## Dive center questions

- Which agencies do you teach?
- What are the differences between agencies?
- How will this affect me?
- How much detail do you go into about the hazards of diving?
- What happens if I can't complete a skill?
- What happens if I need more time to learn a skill?
- What if I decide not to continue, what is your policy on refunds?
- Do you show other equipment configurations like backplate and wing?
- Why should I learn here rather than a nearby dive center?
- What equipment is provided?
- What are my options for the course theory?
- How many students will there be on my course?
- What's the maximum ratio of student to instructor?
- What are the charges for extra tuition?
- Where are the pool sessions held?
- Where do you do the open water dives?
- What happens if a dive is called off?
- What happens if I miss a theory session?
- What are my options for diving with you once certified?

# Useful links

British Sub Aqua Club- https://www.bsac.com/home/
Professional Association of Diving Instructors- https://www.padi.com/
Scuba Schools International- https://www.divessi.com/en-IC/home/
Scuba Diving International- https://www.tdisdi.com/
Dive Raid- https://www.diveraid.com/
World Recreational Scuba Training Council- https://wrstc.com/
WRSTC medical form-
http://wrstc.com/downloads/10%20-%20Medical%20Guidelines.pdf
Global Underwater Explorers-
https://www.gue.com/global-underwater-explorers
Dive Assure- https://diveassure.com/en/home/
Wikipedia list of diving agencies-
https://en.wikipedia.org/wiki/List_of_diver_certification_organizations

# About the author

Richard Devanney is a dive instructor that has previously managed dive centers in Thailand, Iceland, Micronesia, and Indonesia. He has taught recreational diving through PADI, SSI, SDI, BSAC, IANTD, and Raid. He did his open water course with SSI, then PADI advanced, rescue, and divemaster, before becoming a PADI instructor. He then became an instructor with 5 other dive agencies. He currently teaches technical diving with TDI, Raid, SSI, and IANTD.

For fun, he enjoys wreck and cave diving and rebreather diving (owning a JJ-ccr) and furthering his own training with GUE.

He has been lucky to dive and teach in some famously sought after diving locations around the world, notably Truk Lagoon in Micronesia, which was the site of a US air raid against Japanese forces in WWII (Operation Hailstone) and contains the largest concentration of diveable shipwrecks in the world.

For information about other publications written by Richard, visit his website:

https://richarddevanney.com/

He also owns and maintains a website that acts as an information resource for technical divers. He is very active in keeping it up to date with articles on various aspects of diving:

https://bluepo2diving.com/

He has written numerous articles for Technical Diving International, and Scuba Diver Life, an online diving magazine. You can read his articles here:

https://www.tdisdi.com/authors/richard-devanney/
https://scubadiverlife.com/author/richardd/

Made in the USA
Columbia, SC
03 May 2021